AGAINST THE TIDE

3 Monologues for Men
3 Monologues for Women

Stephen Baker

Running time for each monologue
10 - 15 minutes

TSL Drama

Published in Great Britain in 2018
By TSL (Drama) Publications, Rickmansworth

Copyright © 2018 Stephen Baker

Photo by George Hiles on Unsplash

ISBN / 978-1-912416-42-4

Rights of performance

Contents

Ladies Man

Bill is fifty something, divorced and lives alone. The marriage did not produce any children. He is overweight and is seeking a partner, a soul mate. Bill is scruffy. He used to be a cook in the army and now works as a security guard in a supermarket.

Setting

Scene 1 and 3: Armchair
Scene 2: Table and chair

Performance time:

10 minutes

Scene 1

Bill sits in an armchair in his flat.
Clothes drape over the arms of the chair.

Since the divorce I've been missing female company. I think that's an understatement. Never been near a women since the misses walked out on me five years ago. Mental cruelty she said and not enough action between the sheets. Cleared off with some beefcake she met at the gym she did.

Pause.

I've been having a bit of trouble downstairs, you know the waterworks. How embarrassing, gets in the surgery and there's this young girl who's a new locum. Had to explain to her the problem. 'Right let's takes a look,' she said, putting on rubber gloves. 'Drop you trousers and lay on the couch on your side.' I think the least said about what happened next is best all round really. Then if that wasn't enough she only starts quizzing me about my sex life. 'Does it affect your sexual performance?' she asked. I'm flying solo at the moment I said, without thinking, nerves got the better of me and it just slipped out. 'You haven't got a partner at the moment you mean,' she said. Correct I said.

Pause.

Then she starts looking at my notes. 'I see you have a low sperm count,' she said. 'So you haven't been able to start a family.' Well, just because you fire blanks, doesn't mean you can't enjoy yourself on the firing range.

Pause.

And hit the target occasionally.

Pause.

But not frequently enough according to the ex.

Pause.

It was her who made me go to the local clinic for a sperm test. Never been so embarrassed. When I got there a young slip of a girl gave me a bottle and a girlie mag and took me to a cubicle, thankfully with a curtain. 'I'll be back in five minutes,' she said. I know the NHS is short of money but really, a bottle and a girlie mag! And five minutes!

Pause.

Anyway, I've been single for too long. Decided to do something about it. Attended a speed dating event the other night. Things didn't get off to the start that I hoped, but I'm not giving up.

Takes a drink from a mug of coffee.
Pause.

I got a bit nervous just before the event and decided to visit a pub nearby for a bit of 'Dutch courage' as they say. Very common when I was courting in my younger days.

Pause.

Unfortunately I may have had a few too many. I felt a bit tipsy.

Pause.

Anyway, I gets into the venue to be met by this woman with a clip board. She takes my name and points over to some chairs and tells me to take a seat. It was bit like attending the sperm clinic. She then starts reeling off the rules. She points to a screen. 'Behind this screen happiness awaits. There are twenty beautiful ladies each sat individually at a table. You get five minutes with each lady,' she said. Five minutes, I thought, hardly time to get into my stride. 'You then mark on your sheet, which lady you would like to meet again,' she said. All seemed a bit regimental to me. Anyway, she points at me and says, 'Bill you will start at table thirteen.' Well that's a good start I thought, unlucky for some. 'When I blow my whistle, you move onto the next table,' she said. Now I know I've re-enlisted I thought.

Pause.

Whoever said the female of the species is more deadlier than the male got it spot on is all I can say. I sat down at table thirteen as instructed. Turns out my 'first date' is a maternity nurse. We got past the pleasantries of our occupations etc. Then we got onto pastimes. 'What do you do in your leisure time?' she said. Without thinking I said I workout at the local gym. Not been near a gym since I got out of the army but I thought it might impress. She paused and looked at my stomach. 'You can't be doing much on your belly,' she said. And then the killer punch, 'if you visited the maternity hospital where I work, we'd whip you in and induce you.' And laughed out loud. Not sure I saw the funny side really.

Pause.

I didn't fare much better with any of the others. But I ticked all of the tables on my sheet, even the maternity nurse. I always think if you throw enough darts at the at the dart board you're bound to hit the bulls eye eventually.

Pause.

Unfortunately not on this occasion. The woman with the clip board has just rung me to tell me I had no matches, and offered me a free event next week. Think I'll give that one a miss.

Pause.

I need more time to get the patter going, five minutes isn't long enough, think I'll try Internet dating and I am joining a gym to get myself fit. The next date is going to be well impressed when she sees me.

Fades.

Scene 2

Bill sits on a wooden chair in a public house.
There is a table with a half full pint glass.

Well that's Internet dating tried, what a disaster that was. I filled in my details on-line as required. This time I didn't lie, just stretched the truth a little bit to give myself more of a chance. If I knew I'd be dating Miss Marple I wouldn't have bothered.

Pause.

I put in the profile ex-military personnel and currently working in the security business seeks woman into keep-fit. What's wrong with that you may ask? I've joined a gym and got the belly down a bit. (*Points to his stomach*). But it's work in progress, Rome wasn't built in a day. I sent in an oldish photograph but not too old you understand. When I was a bit slimmer. I thought by the time I get to a date I will have slimmed right off.

Pause.

Anyway, I got a response almost straight away from a woman who stated on her profile that she is into keep-fit and wants to meet an 'action man'. Well, I thought, here I am.

Pause.

So I turned up tonight suited and booted. I sat exactly where we had agreed and in walks this fit looking woman and walks straight over to me. 'Is it Bill?' she said. Yes, I said rising to my feet to shake her hand. I saw her gaze centre on my physic. Looking me up and down she was.

Pause.

Would you like a drink? I said. 'Well okay,' she said, 'just an orange juice, I am not sure how long I can stay.'

Pause.

So off I went to the bar. I thought as soon as I get the patter going she'll want to stay all night.

Pause.

When I get back to the table the Spanish Inquisition starts. 'You said you work in security?' she said. 'Where are you based?' Sainsbury's on the High Street, I said. 'When you said you worked in security I assumed you worked for one of the big private companies that hire ex-SAS soldiers to protect their assets overseas,' she said. No I said, I work in the supermarket to ensure no one pinches food off the shelves.

Pause.

And she didn't finish there. 'You said you were in the military,' she said. That's right, I said. 'Army, Navy or RAF,' she said. Army, I said. 'Which Regiment?' she said. Irish Rangers, I said. 'What did you do in the army?' she said. I was the regiment's cook, I said. Batting it back. 'A cook?' she said. 'I came here expecting to meet an Andy McNab, an action man, not Ainsley Harriott,' Well, I said, I think you'll find that Andy McNab and his colleagues need a good meal inside them before they go off doing their heroics. An army marches on its stomach I added. 'Well it's a pity they didn't take you with them,' she snapped, 'maybe you could have lost some of yours.'

Pause.

And then blow me, if she doesn't get up and march off.

Pause.

Women are damn funny nowadays if you ask me. Not sure what I'll do next to meet Miss Right.

Fades.

Scene 3

Bill sits in an armchair in his flat.
Clothes drape over the arms of the chair.

I'm so excited. I have just come back from the Philippines and have met the ideal woman for me. I think someone must be looking out for me. After the disaster of speed and Internet dating, as luck would have it a young woman living in the Philippines decided to contact me after reading my profile. Layla, she's called, said that she knew I was lonely and had viewed my details on-line and felt a real connection.

Pause.

Well I just had to respond. As requested, I sent my personal details, full name, age, etc. She got back to me straight away. Not only did she feel that there was a connection from my first email, but she felt that she was falling in love with me. After what's been happening with British women, I thought to myself Bill you need to give this every opportunity to work.

Pause.

After a few email messages between us, she felt able to tell me that her mother was very sick and needed money for hospital stay. Well I just didn't hesitate. I sent money over straight away. I wanted to show her how caring I am.

Pause.

Then I received a message saying that she wants to meet me, and would I fly over. Yes, I responded. Without hesitation. I booked a flight and a hotel stay with my local travel agent. I've got a bit of money from my army days, invalided out I was, received a pay-off and a pension. So I'm dipping into that to pay

11

for everything. Nothing ventured nothing gained, I always say. Layla stipulated that I book two single rooms as she felt that it was the correct way to go on, until we got to know each other, and she hinted at marriage. So two single rooms it was. I mean I'm no 'smash and grab' merchant. I want to do the right thing and let things develop over a period of time. I don't want to rush things.

Pause.

So, I got to the hotel as planned, and messaged her as she requested. I couldn't believe it when she turned up. Radiant she was. And smart. I've never seen such a stylish dresser. She had a lovely blouse on with a bright yellow neck scarf. She looked radiant. I complimented her on her fashion sense.

Pause.

Everything was going great, we were laughing and enjoying each other's company until her mobile rang; it was the hospital informing that they needed more money before they would give her mother the operation to keep her alive. Well Layla just went to pieces in front of me. Cruel thing to do that. I know I had a bad experience with the NHS but at least our hospitals are free. I immediately agreed to pay for the operation. Well what else could I do? Layla was so grateful. She returned to her old self straight away and accompanied me to the nearest bank to transfer over the money.

Pause.

I met her the next day for breakfast. She was elegantly dressed yet again. Another beautiful blouse and another neck scarf, this time a bright red. Every time I saw her no matter what time of day she had a lovely neck scarf on. I notice these sort of things. I know style when I see it, and she's got style. Must have a full wardrobe of neck scarves.

Pause.

I enjoyed every minute of that holiday I really did. I offered to go to the hospital with her to see her mother, but Layla said no. Which I respected. She said it would be too distressing for the both of us, so she went on her own. That shows she cares about my feelings, unlike the maternity nurse and Miss Marple.

Pause.

Since I've been back Layla's never stopped with her messages. Sometimes she asks for money for her mother convalescing after the operation. Of course I have obliged. With the kindness I've been shown I just can't do anything else.

Pause.

Now Layla is saying she wants to marry me and come and live here in my flat. She just needs to sort out her visa etc. I've just transferred some more money over for this to happen. The accelerated route, Layla called it. She'll be here in no time.

Pause.

Of course, I'll have to spruce this place up a bit. A lick of paint here and there. I'm sure I could sort something out for her mother to come over to stay.

Pause.

I've well and truly done with British women. So, to Florence Nightingale and Miss Marple, you had your opportunity and you blew it (*Points to himself.*), because this guy's taken.

Fades.

Lights down.

The Denby Whites

Brian lives with his wife of five years, Thelma. They have no children. Thelma has been married before, Brian has not. The marriage is going through difficult times.
Brian sits alone in the kitchen.

Setting

Scene 1: Wooden kitchen stool
Scene 2: Chair
Scene 3: Chair

Performance time:

10 minutes

Scene 1

Lights up.

Brian is sitting on a kitchen stool.

It's a truth universally acknowledged, that men don't know how to stack a dishwasher. Try telling the wife that! The dinner party the tonight was going well until the end when I was put on dishwashing duties. She said, 'Where's me Denby Whites? The ones I told you to hand wash as they are delicate.' Her mother bought her the Denby White plates whilst she and hubby were on holiday in Scotland. Not any old plates would do, they had to be the Denby Whites. I must have misheard you I said, knowing what was coming. She said, 'you'd better not've put me Denby Whites in the dishwasher, or you'll be joining them.' We stood and looked at the dishwasher and listened to the strange sounds of it as it went through its cycle.

Pause.

She said, 'My mother brought them all the way from Scotland as a present for me, she did not get them with you in mind. How could she?' But as usual, anything that ends up in your hands perishes! Monica's husband Phillip does all the cooking in their house. She came home last night to Crème Brulee French Toast for a starter, Chicken Cordon Bleu for a main and a Pavlova for dessert. The only thing you can muster is beans on toast.' Philip's one of those men who can turn his hand to anything. Been in the army he has, Special Services. A real action man. The military bring out the best in men I suppose. Me? I didn't get a chance.

Points to his feet.

Flat footed you see. Tried to enlist when I was 17. The sergeant in the recruiting office looked at my feet and said, 'and where do you think you're going with those?' If I'd got in the army I'd be making Crème Brulee French Toast, Chicken Cordon Bleu and a Pavlova for dessert. But we are where we are. I'm not a practical person. A bit clumsy as well due to me dyspraxia. My woodwork teacher use to comment on it. Well not quite in the term I just used. 'You're a walking disaster Wilson,' he used to say, 'If you finish your life with eight fingers and two thumbs, it'll be a bloody miracle.' I think he was referring to the incident with the hand saw.

Noises of plates colliding and doors being slammed can be heard.

The dishwasher incident brought to an end a very eventful evening to say the least! Sandra, or Her Ladyship as I call her, arrived at 6.30. Which is apparently the right time for a dinner date. We had the obligatory kisses on the cheeks. Thelma said, 'Take Sandra's coat upstairs.' Whatever happened to requesting, I asked myself under my breath. I once made the mistake of asking why I get instructions rather than requests. 'Because women organise,' came the response. Don't know why I bothered really. Thelma said, 'Have you set the table as I told you to.' Yes, I said. Of course. Just as I got the words out Her Ladyship shouted from outside where I had placed her on the bench. (*Puts hand to side of mouth.*) She's a little on the large size. She said, 'Brian, this water tastes funny. What was the date on the bottle?' I don't know I said, I didn't look. She said, 'Well can you check?' Only if I went to the recycling bin I said. Thelma intervened, 'I'm sure Brian won't mind having a look at the bottle that he has discarded in the bin.' I recovered the said bottle which gave today's date as the use by. So then we get into a discussion as to whether the use by date means before that date or as I said by the end of the last day. Apparently I was wrong. So out came a new bottle of water. Checked the date and it was in a week's time. Well we all breathed a sigh of relief. Sandra ate most of the nibbles. Thelma said, 'Meal's ready.' Can you show Sandra to her seat.' So I took her through to the dining room. She sat down and straight away said, 'What are we having for the main meal?' Salmon I said. She said, 'So why have I got red wine? I always have a white wine with salmon, a White Rioja usually as per the etiquette.' Thelma shouted through, 'I thought I told you...'

Pause.

The night's disaster unfortunately was not complete. We then had the toilet escapade. Her Ladyship is too big to manage the stairs. Out of breath after only a few steps, so can only use the small downstairs toilet. So apart from all the other duties we had for the day preparing for the royal visit I had to clean the toilet from top to bottom. With a fresh bowl of pot-pourri, and a clean towel. And I was then banned from using it. I could only use the upstairs toilet until Her Ladyship had left the premises. It was bit like being the tradesman sent to repair the dishwasher or something. I'm surprised I wasn't told to come in the back door.

Pause.

Half way through the meal Her Ladyship decided she wanted to use the loo. Up she got moving her enormous carcass. I wondered how the toilet was going to take the weight. And I wonder who'd be given the job of cleaning up the mess if the bowl came away from the floor. (*Scratches his head.*) Um, let's think about that one. But that wasn't the mishap. If it was, at least I couldn't have been blamed. She only got trapped in the toilet! Thelma said, 'Sandra has been a long time, I'm going to investigate, you stay there.' I suddenly remembered something rather important. Thelma had given me a list of instructions for the day in preparation for the visit of Her Ladyship. One of the tasks was to oil the latch on the downstairs toilet door. I forgot. Please don't let Thelma come through and say Sandra is trapped in the toilet.

I murmured to myself, the bowl coming away from the floor would be far better for me. No sooner had I got the words out when Thelma came rushing through looking stressed and the words came out of her mouth like a Gatling gun, 'Sandra is trapped in the toilet, the latch that you were supposed to oil is stuck. Is there anything at all that you can do that has a positive outcome?' I've learnt not to answer rhetorical questions from Thelma, even in jest. I walked over to the door. Sandra, I said push the door towards me and lift the latch at the same time. Good clear instructions I thought. 'I am doing that and it's not working,' came the flustered response. After about half an hour of trial and error we managed to get her freed. The look on Thelma's face when I went to get the can of oil from the garage. Stood there with hands on hips, just like my female boss does, when I have done something wrong.

Pause.

Our marriage problem became exacerbated after visiting a marriage councillor. Her idea it was. As usual I didn't get a say. She said, 'We're going to a marriage guidance councillor. It's Tuesday week at 6.30, so don't go arranging anything else'. Nice to be asked I said sarcastically. Big mistake. She said, 'I've spent the last five years of my life consulting you on everything and look where it's got me.' Always good at rhetorical questions the wife. 'Nowhere,' we both said in unison.

Pause.

It was about the third session with Chloe the marriage councillor, nice girl, but very young. Not sure what experience she has in relationships. She said to Thelma, 'What issue do you have with Brian?' Just like that. You could have knocked me down with a feather. 'Not very good around the house,' came the reply. Chloe said, 'Can you be more specific.' Thelma said, 'The kitchen and the bedroom seem to be areas of concern.' Trust her to link the relationship to rooms of the house. Only she could do that. Areas of concern, sounds like something that was put on my school report, but then Thelma is a school teacher. 'He can't cook and he is totally unimaginative in the bedroom.' came the immediate response.

Pause.

Anyway to cut a long story short. Chloe recommended that we try the two week challenge. Which basically means we have sex every day for two weeks anywhere in the house except the bedroom and it doesn't matter how long it lasts. Thelma had to put the damper on things straight away. She looked at me and said, it's the two week challenge not the two minute challenge.' Always has to have the last word does Thelma.

Fade out.

Scene 2

Lights up.

Brian sits on a bedside chair.

Thelma's got Her Ladyship round for coffee and cake. Miss know it all. I've no doubt she finds out today that the two week challenge has being suspended. We might as well put a message in the local paper: Thelma and Brian wish to inform all those interested that the two week challenge has been suspended until further notice. We're taking advantage of a pit stop for a tyre change.

Chloe said anywhere anytime for as long as you like for two weeks. I always fancied the sun room for a bit of love making, it's got a television with TV on demand. So I thought, Brian use a bit of imagination. I've been watching that 'Naked Attraction' on Channel 4 on a Thursday night at 10.00 whilst the wife's at her kitchen skills class, doesn't get home until 11.00; strange time to have a cookery class if you ask me. Gets back really tired as well and straight to bed and asleep by the time I come up, which is a bit of a problem if you see what I mean.

Anyway, It always has a guy on first and he chooses a date from six naked women. If you can't choose a date from six women with their kit off there something wrong somewhere. He whittles it down to two and then he gets his kit off. And after the adverts a girl comes on and she chooses a date after whittling the field down. She gets her kit off before choosing her guy. I always make a coffee during the break. As you do.

Anyway, I hit on the idea of suggesting watching the pro-gramme the day after its screening, thought it would be nice to kick start things. So there we were sat in the sun lounge and on comes the programme. The presenter says 'And meet Dominic who is eager to find a date.' Fantastic I thought, here we go six birds in the buff no problem, and when he gets his kit off we'll be well away. Well you could have knocked me down with a feather. He was only a gay boy. Six blokes in the buff. Thelma looked at me and I looked at her. She said, 'So this is what you watch whilst I'm out.' And just to make matters worse we don't have the facility to fast forward. I made a cup of coffee and we sat and waited until the second bit when a girl called Laura came to choose her date. Right fit looking piece can't wait until she whittles them down and gets her kit off before choosing the lucky guy. Six great big hunks she had to choose from.

Well we got to the last bit with her stood naked next to the last two guys and we got at it. Who knows who she chose? And who cares? Onto the burgundy rug we went. It must have been the sight of the six naked beefcakes that did it. Thelma was like a wild animal. She climbed on top and was riding away. Usually my planning is first class. I had planned to do a grand tour of the house. Chloe had said stay out of the bedroom, utilise all the other rooms. I just forgot that the Sun Room is used by the cat. He likes to snuggle up in his igloo. As the saying goes: curiosity killed the cat, or in this case the passion. Let's just say the distraction of having my face licked caused a bit of a problem down below.

Pause.

I thought of including the garage on the grand tour of the house but then I remembered the wonky shutter. Keeps going up on its own accord. Nearly gave me heart attack the first time it happened. And we don't want to frighten the neighbours do we? Especially Mr Harrison opposite with his pacemaker. Actually it may even be Mr Harrison with his pacemaker who's causing the problem, he always seems to be around when it happens. The next room had to be the kitchen. I waited until we'd had our meal and washed up, it was with some trepidation I reminded Thelma that we were on the second day of the two week challenge. Well if looks could kill. She said, 'In case you have forgotten I am going through the change and am on HRT. Not that you take any notice. And I've got better things to do than satisfy your needs, I'm arranging the Denby Whites for the next dinner date.' Well wouldn't you just know it. Me, Denby Whites, only one winner. So for the two week challenge we've managed to rack up one session. I feel like the opening batsman who only scored one run and is looking forward to the second innings to make amends. But will there be a second innings? I ask myself.

Glances out the window.

The only sexual stimulation I get at the moment is the sight of the neighbour hanging her underwear out. Very nice, looks like lace from here. I wonder if her and her hubby do the two week challenge. She might, but not sure about him, he works away you see. Long distance lorry driver I think. Only comes home at weekends. The bloke from the across the road visits Monday to Friday. Not sure if the two week challenge covers three people in the equation. When Chloe explained the benefits of the challenge, I distinctly remember her saying it's meant to bring the couple much closer together. Still I bet when hubby does come home at the weekend he doesn't have to put up with the middle class dinner dates like I've had to. Working class that's the class to be, you get your dinner on your lap and watch TV. None of this nonsense with napkins and cutlery from the special drawer. I bet her hubby isn't sent to the garage for the Piello Chardonnay. It'll be a can of lager from the fridge or a bottle of plonk from Tesco if they're pushing the boat out.

Pause.

It's a bit like being a teenager again really, but without the sex. I've got my own room and I'm getting grief every day for being untidy and not helping around the house. I half expect my mother to burst through the door any minute and bollock me for not tidying my room. Strange how I've managed to go full circle.

Pause.

I wonder how they're getting along downstairs. I wonder if the Denby Whites' escapade has been mentioned yet. Probably the first topic of conversation I expect.

Pause.

I suppose all of my failings will be explored and scrutinised. I bet it won't be mentioned that I had to visit the DIY store after one of Her Ladyship's visits; to purchase industrial nuts and bolts so that I could strengthen the bench on the decking after she nearly broke it by sitting on it. The bolts were almost bent in two. The very bench where she sat outside and devoured the nibbles.

Fade.

Scene 3

Lights up.

Brian sits on a wooden chair.

Well that's the two week challenge well and truly out the window, so to speak. Thelma's booted me out. She said, 'The relationship has run its course.' So all the work Chloe put in with her two week challenge proposal, all to no avail. Moved into a boarding house for the time being. No more dinner dates, Piello Chardonnay and napkins.

Pause.

Not quite the standard that one is use to, and that's putting it mildly. I wasn't exactly expecting the Denby Whites when I went down for breakfast this morning or napkins placed delicately in front of the guests, but really, is this how people live? The plates might have been white at some stage, but the ones I was expected to eat my breakfast on were a very odd yellow colour and the table cloth had not been cleaned after the previous diner. Social etiquette doesn't seem to exist, elbows on the table and tea slurped rather than drank. I guess this is what they call slumming it.

Pause.

Bit of a change on the shopping front. Goodbye Waitrose, hello Co-op. Bit of a come down. Whilst Phillip's shopping in Waitrose for ingredients for his Crème Brulee French Toast, Chicken Cordon Bleu and Pavlova, I'm buying ready meals for one. In football terms I've been relegated. I'm playing in the lower division. It's the division of ready meals and soups. No more shopping with Thelma for the next dinner date. No more pushing the trolley with Thelma and her list, stopping at every isle. 'Can you see the Mascarpone cheese?' she would say. 'And what shall we have for nibbles? Nuts or those nice cheese biscuits we had last time?'

Now it's the ready meal isle. Great big sign hanging over the isle 'Ready Meals'. They might as well call it the Singleton's Isle. I'm there basket in hand with all the other single blokes. Finance dictates our spending habits. No more expensive plonk for Brian. No, will be lucky if I can afford the £7 a bottle of wine offer.

And if it's not bad enough shopping on your own down the singleton isle, when you attempt to go the tills you get directed to the self-checkout or worse, the small item check-out. It comes as dictat from the floor supervisor, always a middle aged woman with a permanent smile on her face. She takes one look at my basket and says, 'I think you need to be at the small item check-out.' And there laid bare on the conveyer belt is a statement of your life: small tin of beans, small carton of milk, small loaf (if you get a normal size it will go off by the time you get round to eating it) and the dreaded ready meal for one. Says it all really.

Phillip will be at Waitrose at the check-out for bakers and cooks, his ingredients for his Pavlova on display for everyone to see, the best eggs on the shelf. Nothing less will do. No ready meals for him, strange how he and Thelma always seem to have identical shopping lists.

Pause.

I wonder what Thelma's doing whilst I'm in here, probably still doing her coffee and cake meetings with her friends no doubt. Very popular with friends and neighbours she is. Always receiving texts at the last minute she was, inviting her to this and that. Friends just popping through and texting to meet up for coffee and cake in the adjacent village, and off she'd go. It's a wonder she never put any weight on all the coffee and cake she consumed. And then there were all the meetings in the village with various people. Who ever said village life was quiet doesn't know what they are talking about. Always rushing off to people's houses in the village to discuss matters to do with the parish council. She deserves a plaque for the all the effort she has put into council matters. An unsung hero is Thelma, an unsung hero.

Pause.

I wonder if we'd managed to do a bit more on the two week challenge if we'd been able to resolve the relationship problems. We only managed one room, before she called a halt to proceedings.

Pause.

No more waiting on her Ladyship.

Pause.

No more dishwasher stacking.

Pause.

No more of Philip's Crème Brullee French toast, Chicken Cordon Bleu, Pavlova and Piello Chardonnay.

Pause.

No more toilet cleaning duties and pot-pourri.

Pause.

No more placing the Denby Whites delicately on the dining table, wine to the right, port to the left.

Pause.

Went to a restaurant last night, was greeted by the waitress, she said, 'How many for sir?' I said, table for one.

Fades out.
Lights down.

These Mean Streets

Terry is 58 years old. He lives with his wife, Rosie who is the same age. They live in a quite village called Horkston, population 105. Terry is semi re-tired and works part-time for the local authority as a library assistant. He is bored with his life and dreams of some excitement. Both he and Rosie are well travelled having visited many different countries. They have just come back from a holiday in New York.

Setting

Scene 1: Armchair and New York picture
Scene 2 and 3: Wooden kitchen chair
Scene 4: Wooden chair

Performance time:

15 minutes

Scene 1

Lights up.

Terry sits in an armchair.
A picture of New York hangs behind him.

Well, we've just come back from New York. What a place that is. It used to be the crime capital of the States, until the new mayor got elected. Zero crime tolerance, that's the ticket he got elected on. None of this nonsense of let's give them another chance. Lock em up and throw away the key. That's his motto. When we went there a few years ago you couldn't walk down the street without the fear of being mugged. Now armed police are everywhere patrolling, usually in twos. Rosie was very impressed by the police presence. Everywhere we went she was always looking to see how many police officers were patrolling. It was a security thing. She needed to feel re-assured.

Pause.

It was the experience of New York that gave Rosie an idea for myself. I've been a bit restless as of late; only working part-time and having a lot of time on my hands. And I have a great respect for law and order and she came up with a great idea. 'You should start up a neighbourhood watch group,' she said. Well I thought, what an excellent idea. I've kept silent for long enough with the lawlessness in the village. People not respecting other people's property. I spoke to Mrs Gown in the post office the other day, absolutely distressed she was, someone had taken it upon themselves to open her front gate go onto her garden and flatten her newly planted flower bed. It sounds like an act of sabotage to me, the annual village best garden competition is just around the corner.

Pause.

It's behaviour like that which needs to be stamped out, and quickly, if you pardon the pun. And I'm just the man to do it. One minute it's flower bed stamping, the next thing you know it's armed robbery. Zero tolerance, that's what it's all about; and I have zero tolerance.

Pause.

Rosie soon puts things in motion. She sits on the parish council. I was sat next to her in the kitchen when she rang the clerk and put it on the agenda, for the setting up of a neighbourhood watch, with yours truly as the chair; and as soon as she put the phone down she immediately rang the vice chair, Will, who is an ex major in the army. Discipline and all that, one of the 'old school'. He likes people who share his views on law and order. Rosie explained what she had done and asked if he would support me as the chair and second her proposal. No sooner had she asked then her face lit up and she gave me a thumbs up. I was so excited. I felt a new vigour, and I took myself into the garden and mowed the lawn dreaming of my new role and all I was going to achieve.

Pause.

I couldn't attend the parish council meeting the following week as I had to work at the library. Those books don't stack themselves. I just couldn't wait for the shift to end. My supervisor said, 'Terry I don't know what's happening in your life, but you just seem a million miles away.' In some ways she was right, I just couldn't stop thinking about my new role. Subject to parish council parish council approval that is.

Pause.

I couldn't have my mobile phone with me for my shift, library rules and all that. I just had to wait until I got home to find out what had happened.

Gets all excited.

I ran through into the house and there on the table was a bottle of wine and two glasses. Rosie was sat at the table with a great big smile on her face. I thought you'd like to celebrate in style,' she said. It went through? I asked. 'Not only did it go through,' she said, 'but Will has offered to chip in a few bob to pay for a uniform for you.'

Pause.

Well you could have knocked me down with a feather. A uniform. He's worth a bit is Will, owns a few properties in the village. Well I say a few, most of the village actually. Not our modest little bungalow, but most of the other properties. So he'll not want the village becoming a hotbed for crime. And being a business man he's a very good judge of character. He knows someone who will do a job. Step forward me, Terry Fewlass Crime Tsar of Horkston.

Pause.

Fades.

Scene 2

Lights up.

Terry sits astride a wooden chair in the kitchen.

He is dressed all in blue, in a t-shirt and combat trousers with a baseball cap.

Well as you can see, Will was true to his word. He just turned up at the door with a bag containing my new uniform. He insisted that I put it on straight away. He had a camera with him. He explained that he had started a Facebook page dedicated to the village Neighbourhood Watch and he wanted to take some pictures of me in the uniform so everyone knew who was responsible for keeping the village safe. It's not the police, I know that. Never see them with all the cuts. They're all in the big towns and cities, that's why people like me need to step up and take the initiative. Criminals needn't look at Horkston for their next crime.

Pause.

I hurriedly got changed. I felt like a child again when my mother came home with my new school uniform. I couldn't wait to put it on. I was wearing it long before the start of the school term. There's something about a uniform. It gives you respect. (He puffs his chest out.) I've always had a sense of responsibility too, I was a milk monitor at school. You can always rely on me.

Pause.

Anyway, back to my new role. Will suggested that we go into the garden and he took pictures. He knows how to get the message across, does Will. He said, 'Fold your arms and look mean. People need to know what they're dealing with.' Then he suggested that we go into the village for some action shots. I was so excited. Off we went.

Pause.

There I was stood outside the post office, the scene of an attempted bicycle theft only last week. Will gets me to point at the cycle rack. Snap. He was going to write the caption on Facebook later, something dynamic, you know the sort of thing, 'Terry is on the case, no stone left unturned.' Everyone was looking, it was great. Some idiot in a tractor passing through shouted, 'Go ahead punk, make my day,' which seemed to amuse everyone stood at the bus stop. Anyway they should be grateful someone is prepared to stand up for the community, whilst they're sleeping safely in their beds, I'll be patrolling the streets.

Pause.

I've already got my first case to work on. I'm on friendly terms with a governor at the local primary school. There's a pair of twin boys in Year 2, six year olds they are. Been playing up by all accounts, back chatting the teachers etc, etc. The school decided to give them some responsibility. They put them in charge of the tuck shop. And how did they repay the school? Well I'll tell you. They pocketed half the proceeds is what they did. It was only through the sharpness of one of the young teachers that their little crime was uncovered. She noticed a flurry of activity at the shop but the takings were down. Just like me she's got a nose for crime. If these two aren't dealt with the next thing you know they'll be running a crime syndicate in the village. Well not whilst I've got anything to do with it, they won't. I made a note in my diary to arrive at the school gates one morning and speak to the mother and maybe the teacher, as I could do with a deputy.

Pause.

So as promised first thing in the morning I set off for the school on my trusty bicycle. I see the mother with her two boys. I waited for them to go into school. Don't want to make them late. I approached mother and explained who I was and why I needed to speak to her. We entered into dialogue. You need to exercise some parental control, I said. 'And you need to piss off,' she said.

Pause.

Charming, I thought. But I'm not going to be deterred. The fight against crime continues. Do you think Clint Eastwood in Carmel, Arnie in California and Giluiani in New York haven't been sworn at? Of course they'll have. When you're fighting crime, it goes with the territory.

Pause.

In the words of Arnie (*Gets up from the chair.*), I'll be back.

Walks towards the door.

Fade.

Scene 3

Lights up.

(To the tune of the Z Car theme tune.) Terry appears from a door. Dressed in his uniform. Sporting a black eye.

Terry touches the brim of his cap.

Evening All. (*Sits down in his chair, in his usual pose.*) I expect you're wondering how I got this little beauty. (*Points to his black eye.*) Well I'll tell you. Doing my job is how I got this.

Reaches in his trouser back pocket and retrieves a notebook.

I was on the day shift patrol walking along the track that runs along the river bank at approximately 0900 hours. I noticed in the distance one I C 1 female. That's one white women for those not familiar with police speak. She was walking a dog off the lead. I hid behind a bush, didn't want to be seen, I needed to get evidence for prosecution. Someone had messaged on the Facebook page that someone was letting their dog foul the path without picking it up.

Pause.

Gets up, re-enacts movements as he speaks before sitting down again.

I waited binoculars and camera at the ready. And Bingo. Got yer, I thought. I took photographs as evidence. I jumped out of the bush and proceed in the direction of the woman to confront her. She spots me, shouts to the dog, 'Hugo.' Great I thought, I've now got a name. Then she starts to walk at a hurried pace.

Never give up. That's my motto. The police officer who investigated the great train robbery was known as Slipper of the Yard. He didn't give up either, he was still tracking down the culprits twenty years later. You have to be resilient in this game.

Pause.

Anyway, I followed her to the next village, Bodby. Not my patch you understand. But even in the States, a crime fighter crosses the border into the next State if they are in pursuit of a criminal. She hurries down a path to her house. I wasn't giving up on this. I decided I was going to write the address down and report her to the Environmental Health Department at the local authority. So, there I was, stood outside of the said house, notebook in hand. I could see the curtain moving and the guilty party looking through the window. Next thing the front door opens and a male came out, I assumed to be the husband.

Pause.

I was just about to explain my actions and indeed what action I was going to make; when I was punched in the eye. He said something about a pervert. I said, I patrol the villages and I can assure you I am not aware of any perverts. I must check the Facebook page when I get home. If someone is annoying women I need to know about it. This is moving up a gear. This is the big time.

Pause.

Even though I had been assaulted, I was still thinking of my role of crime fighter. I decided that I just had to contact my opposite number in Bodby and inform him that he has a pervert on his patch and a violent individual to deal with.

Pause.

So I set off home. Well my impromptu appearance ruined a surprise that Rosie had for me. She saw my injury and immediately made a fuss. You know what women are like. Out came the first aid box and the steak that was planned for tea was placed over my eye. No the steak for tea wasn't the surprise.

Pause.

Whilst being generally pampered. I noticed that the postman had been and delivered a rather large parcel. It was draped over the chair in the sun room. What's that? I asked. 'Oh, it's a surprise,' she said. 'You weren't meant to see it.' Well she's not going to keep any secrets from me is she? Not with my background. I never leave a stone unturned. She said, 'Well if you must know, it's a garment that I have got you to wear for the village fancy dress. The surprise is ruined now.' Well the excitement got the better of me. I pestered her to open it.

Pause.

'Close your eyes,' she said. So, I did. I could hear the wrapping paper being opened. 'Open them,' she said. I opened them and there staring at me was a New York Police Department's uniform. 'Do you like it?' she asked. Do I like it? I love it, I said. I can't wait to wear it. 'Well you're not wearing it yet. You'll have to wait a month until the fancy dress party. I'm putting it away,' she said.

Pause.

Anyway, going back to crime fighting, after a bit of activity on the computer, tipping off my opposite number in Bodby, about recent events. I decided not to report the assault to the police. I thought that it would undermine moral in the village if people knew that the main crime fighter had been the victim of a crime himself.

Pause.

And to emphasise my dedication to fighting crime, I have decided to do the night shift. I've been made aware via the Facebook page of incidents of disturbance at throwing out time at the village public house, The Fox and Hounds. So, I intend to cycle down there tonight and speak to the culprits myself. Of course, Rosie was worried, especially after the morning's incident. But she knows that I am determined to crack down on anything that affects the lives of people in the village.

Pause.

So there I am getting the bicycle out of the garage. When out comes Rosie, with a flask. 'I've made you a hot drink,' she says.

And make sure you remove your bicycle clips from your trousers, before you confront anyone.' Honestly, women! I bet Clint doesn't have a woman fussing over him when he's out there fighting crime.

Fades.

Scene 4

Lights up.

Terry sits on a wooden chair in a bed and breakfast establishment.

You may be wondering what I am doing in this grubby bed and breakfast. Probably you're thinking he must be on an 'oppo' dressed in civies. Well if you are thinking that, then I'm afraid you couldn't be more wrong. I've given up crime fighting, I've hung up my uniform for good; gone into permanent retirement.

Pause.

So what has brought about this sudden change of direction? You may ask. Well it wasn't the assault or the verbal abuse. It was something that occurred on the evening of the visit to the public house. No I didn't get abused or assaulted, but my pride has been severely hurt.

Pause.

I set off on my bicycle as planned at 22.00 hours, had everything that I would need in my backpack, or so I thought. I decided beforehand that I would lock my bicycle to the rack and take a look around before hiding in the bushes to catch the rowdy culprits who have been making life difficult for those living nearby with the constant noise. Totally unnecessary if you ask me. When I come out of a pub you can hear a pin drop.

Pause.

I had been informed that teenagers were gathering in the woods at the back of the post office, illegal drinking that sort of thing. Kill two birds with one stone. Anyway to have a look around at that time of night you need a good torch. And I have one, Rosie bought me one for such a task. Unfortunately, when I searched my bag for it, it was not there, gloves, flask, notebook, but no torch. Not very helpful really. I bet when Jack 'Slipper' of the yard went out on a night looking for clues as to who committed the great train robbery he had a torch. Well I didn't. So, I had to make a decision. Should I stay or go back home for the torch. I decided on the latter.

Pause.

So I cycled home and intended to leave my bicycle on the drive whilst I nipped in the garage for my torch. When I got to the house I noticed Will's Range Rover on the drive. I thought, funny time to be calling. He does often does call round to inform me of things going on in the village. He gets little tip-offs from anonymous sources. Then I follow up those leads. Team work and all that.

Pause.

Anyway, I went into the kitchen and no one was there. I thought maybe Rosie has taken him to the study upstairs. I walked up the stairs and could hear noises coming from our bedroom. The door was slightly ajar. So I peered in. All I can say on what I saw, is that the New York Police Department uniform was never intended for me, and there was a pair of handcuffs that went with it!

Pause.

According to neighbours it had been going on for some time. Everybody knew apparently – that is except the one person whose job it was to find out what was going on in the village. No wonder they both were eager for me to form the Neighbourhood Watch. It was to get me out of the way.

Gets up from the chair.

This time in the words of Terry Fewlass: I won't be back.

Walks towards the door.

Fades to lights down.

Everyone Loves Tony

Ruth is in her early forties and married to Tony who is nearing his sixties. Ruth is a newly promoted head teacher of a primary school but has worked at the same school for five years. The school,an academy, was rated excellent at the last Ofsted inspection. She and her deputy Helen were the only internal candidates for the post of head teacher. Ruth feels that Helen bears a grudge against her and is undermining her position.

Setting

Scene 1 and 3: Armchair
Scene 2: Desk and chair

Performance time:

10 minutes

Scene 1

Lights up.

Ruth sits in an armchair at home. She has her glasses on a chain, they sit neatly perched on her nose.

Problem solving. That's always been my strong point, as I reiterated to the school governors at my interview for the post of head teacher. I was asked to demonstrate my problem solving abilities. I just reeled off the long list from my educational history.

Pause.

Then I'm straight into my post and a problem arises. The lazy caretaker burst into my office with yet more demands. I refused to concede, one of my strong points is that I don't give an inch. Being a constant thorn in the backside that one. Well he met his match in me, I can tell you, and I'm not like my predecessor, always giving in. Anyway, he took his bat home and went sick. Typical.

Pause.

My deputy went into a right paddy about it. 'Who is going to open up in the morning,' she wailed. Fear not young lady I said. I have just the answer.

Pause.

As luck would have it. Tony my hubby, has just left his job at the paint factory. They just didn't appreciate him. He left to pursue other interests as the saying goes. He's not been very lucky in work. He was between jobs when I met him and I had to pull a few strings to get him the job at the paint factory. The manager there is the father of one of the pupils. Anyway their loss is our gain; I seized the opportunity and appointed him the temporary caretaker. I rang him to tell him the good news, he was over the moon, as they say in football. Over the moon. I told him he could start in the morning.

Pause.

I stopped at the local DIY store on the way home and bought him a super tool box. You should have seen his face when I gave it to him. He was like a child in a sweet shop for the first time. He was so excited, he took every tool out separately looking in amazement at it before putting it down and picking up another.

Pause.

Of course Helen my deputy had to say something about the appointment. 'You have to go through the proper channels,' she said. Nonsense, I said, we are an academy and I think you'll find that I have ultimate authority. That told her.

Pause.

Tony started in the morning, as intended, 6.30 to be precise. Very important to get there early to put the heating on, can't have the little dears starting the day cold.

Pause.

I was inundated by teachers with praise. He can't do enough for us was what they were all saying. Hanging doors, putting up shelves, carrying books. You name it, he does it. What an appointment I've made. I feel like Alex Ferguson making a vital substitution in the last few minutes of an important game. We are big Manchester United fans. I said to him and don't go acting like one of the substitutes warming up before Ferguson brings him on. I've seen them spitting all over and pulling at their shorts before putting their hands down there, checking what they've got. I said you can run up the sports touch line if you want, but don't go messing with the crown jewels. Don't want the kids picking up bad habits.

Pause.

It's plain to see, everyone loves Tony. Especially Laura the new teacher. One of my appointments I might add. She thinks the world of Tony, He's always helping her, bringing stuff from her car. Anything really.

Pause.

The exception is Helen. Always got a bee in her bonnet that one. Never forgiven me for beating her to the post. Well maybe she should brush up on her problem solving skills instead of burying her head in the policy books, which are on my shelves gathering dust. I'm sure I'll get round to reading them some day. But at the moment I am rather busy running a school.

Pause.

And as reward for all his hard work, I am taking him out tonight for a special celebratory meal at the restaurant in the nearby village.

Pause.

Everyone Loves Tony.

Fades.

Scene 2

Lights up.

Ruth sits behind a desk, her glasses on the end of her nose.

Well what a week it's been. Very challenging I must say. We went out for the meal as planned. Tony insisted on driving rather than get a taxi. He wanted to be back to watch Match of the Day. United were on. He didn't want to miss the start, and he didn't trust the taxi firm to arrive on time. But he ended up missing the football after all, because the police were doing a speed check as we got out of the village and stopped him for speeding. Then they breathalysed him and said he was over the limit. Treated like a criminal he was. Only spent the night in the cells. And worse was to come he has lost his licence. Well he is appealing that one. Slightly over maybe, but not enough to deserve losing his licence. I shall be writing to the Chief Constable, as I would like to know how somebody with a clean licence can be removed from the road for their first offence; whatever happened to the speed seminars and common sense? The restaurant have to take some of the blame, the waiter kept coming back and topping up our glasses. We didn't like to say no.

Pause.

And of course Helen is lapping it up. 'How is Tony going to open up in a morning?' she said. I shall be bringing him, I said. 'So are you bringing him at 6.30 in the morning?' she said, 'so that he can fire up the boilers to get the heating on for when the pupils get here at 8.00am for the breakfast club.' No. I said I will be bringing him for the time being at 8.00am until his appeal is heard and this nonsense is sorted out. 'And what about the kids, it's the middle of winter?' she said. Get them to jump about a bit

I said. That told her, she stormed out of my office. Got an attitude problem that one.

Pause.

And next thing I knew back she came again, this time to tell me about a shelf that had fallen down. She said, 'Mrs Cooper the maths teacher was half way through her lesson when there was banging and clattering, as a shelf fell off the wall and all the books ended up on the floor.' Well maybe Mrs Cooper should take greater care in how many books she puts on the shelf. I said. Never thinks that woman.

Pause.

And I just get settled down to write the progress report for the governors, when blow me if Helen doesn't burst into my office again waving the first aid book. 'We have just had a serious accident near the plant room,' she said. "Millie Watson has just gone flying, she stood in a pool of oil that had been left on the floor and went hurtling into a table.' Well maybe she shouldn't have been running the first place I said. Always on the go that girl, got far too much energy if you ask me. I must make a note to have her looked at, I wonder if she's got that attention disorder.

Pause.

Helen took a breath and said, 'Isn't it about time...' I stopped her full in her tracks. Don't you even go there, I said. I am inundated with teachers (*Points at the door.*) walking through that door praising him. Everyone loves Tony.

Pause.

So, I just get settled down again when the secretary puts a call through from the chair of governors, John Franks. 'I'm hearing on the grapevine that all is not well at the school,' he said. Let me put your mind at rest there, I said. Everything is running just fine. Couldn't be better. 'What about all these incidents,' he said. And he started to go on about the shelf and the building being cold in a morning, blah, blah, blah. And we know where he got that from. Had to reassure him that all was well. And that all those on temporary appointments would have to apply for that position in an open and transparent process. Just to please the Union of course. It's a juggling exercise all of us heads have to go through. We have the government saying do this and the unions saying do that. What I do is what's best for the children and the school. John didn't mention anyone's name but we all know who he was referring to and where he got his little snippets of information from. I shall deal with Helen one of these days, I really will. Just like that lazy so and so the old caretaker. There's a line in the sand with me and you cross it at your peril. Don't get me wrong, I'm not a tyrant. I just expect people to do the job that they have been employed to do. No more, no less. We are all here for the benefit of the children. Not for ourselves, just for the children; and some people just don't seem to grasp that. And one of my many roles is to see that they do.

Pause.

I went to find Tony to let him know about all the kafuffle. He wasn't in his office, but the why would he be? He'd be in the building doing repairs. And just as I thought he was. I finally tracked him down to Laura's class room. The door had come off its hinges and he was fixing it. I knew he'd be doing something constructive and helping someone. Everyone loves Tony.

Pause.

Everything okay? I asked, looking at Laura. Knowing what the reply would be. 'Absolutely,' she said. 'Tony is so helpful, the door keeps coming off its hinges. This is the third time Tony has had to come and repair it. He is so helpful. Not like the other caretaker we had who could never be bothered.' Just the response I knew I would get. She'll go places that young lady, you mark my words. She'll go places will that one.

Fades.

Scene 3

Lights up.

Ruth sits in an armchair at her home.

Terry is having a bit of a lie down upstairs. He's had a bit of a tipple if you see what I mean. Anyone who works as hard as he does deserves to let their hair down occasionally, I say. He likes to celebrate, Manchester United winning that sort of thing, and if he has had a hard day at work, and let's face it in this line of work every day is a hard day.

Well let's reflect on the last day as us head teachers say. The morning started with Mr Williams the sports teacher waiting for me outside of my office. 'I need to speak to you about last night,' he said in his broad Welsh accent. Oh Yes Mr Williams, what about last night, I said. 'The under 11's got knocked out of the cup is what happened last night,' he said. Well that's hardly a catastrophe of biblical proportions Mr Williams I said.

Pause.

He then decided to give a running commentary on the opposition's last and deciding goal. He got that excited I almost called for an interpreter. It seems that one their players was running down the wing, and may have crossed over the touchline, before crossing the ball for their centre forward to head into the net. When I finally got him to calm down I managed to establish that the dispute was over a wonky touchline. Apparently the line had not been drawn in a straight line and the winger took advantage of the extra width and managed to escape a tackle in the process.

Pause.

He gets very excited does Mr Williams. He's a Manchester City fan. Never forgiven us for the drubbing we gave them at their ground only last month. Of course Tony and I were there, in the corporate boxes of course; courtesy of the academy. I said, I think we need to get things in proportion, it was hardly the FA Cup. And of course that got him, as the match between United and City had been the Quarter Final of the FA Cup. He didn't seem to like the jibe about the FA Cup.

Pause.

He just stood there mouth open but nothing coming out. I decided to go for the jugular.

  And what would you like me to do about this grave injustice? I said. Spend thousands of pounds from the school budget on a video referee? I suggested very sarcastically; and invite Gary Lineker and Alan Shearer round to give their analysis. 'No,' he said, 'get your husband to draw a bloody touchline straight.' And then if he didn't just storm off down the corridor. So that's two who won't have Tony on their Christmas card list.

Pause.

Honestly some people. They don't know a grafter when they see one. Everyone loves Tony.

Pause.

And if that wasn't enough I then had to deal with the fire brigade. Well when I say the fire brigade, I mean the chief fire officer. At about 2.pm the fire alarm sounded. I was due to do a fire drill anyway. So it saved me a task. It turned out we had a little fire in the plant room. And Tony was there to put it out. You can always rely on Tony. Always doing something. Everyone loves Tony.

Pause.

So we end up with the cavalry. Fire engines everywhere. No wonder public finances are stretched. Firemen all over the building. Some of the young female teachers took the opportunity to flirt. Men in uniforms, always a weakness for the younger generation. Plenty of cleavages on display if you see what I mean. Well I don't miss a trick. I soon put a stop that to that. Everyone was evacuated onto the playing field as per the procedure. I don't know what all the fuss was about. The fire wardens did their job. Job well done as far as I am concerned.

Pause.

The Chief Fire Officer makes a bee line for me. Long story short. Apparently, a valve in the plant room was open when it should have been closed, and it caused the filter to overheat and catch fire. The fire officer was concerned that it was due to human error, and we all know who was responsible for that, he's sat at home on sick. It's a good job Tony was there to put the fire out. From the school's point of view everything went smoothly, except for the exposed bosoms, the fire wardens organised all the children getting them out of harm's way. The evacuation procedure was effected immaculately. (*Ruth puts one hand to the side of her mouth.*) Modesty prevents me from saying who re-wrote the fire evacuation procedure.

Pause.

Of course the fire officer had to go on and on about it, a right jumped up little Hitler he was if you ask me. He said he would be contacting the Chief Executive of the academy. He should be grateful that Tony did their job for them, I wish someone would come into the school and do my job for me. And also he should be thankful that we gave them the practice they need for dealing with a real emergency. Practice makes perfect, as my mother used to say.

Pause.

I was just sat at my desk late in the afternoon after all the commotion; and I was thinking, I hope the chair of governors and the chief executive of the academy appreciate all the hard work I do, and, let's not forget the effort of others. Even though I have only been in the job a short while, I feel that I am ready for a new challenge. I feel that I have outgrown operational management already.

Pause.

And then blow me, the school secretary came in to the office with a message from the chair of governors. She'd written it down and slipped it onto my desk. It was marked urgent. Basically, the Chair and the Chief Executive of the academy are coming to the school first thing in the morning to meet with me. And wait for it, I am to leave my keys with Helen my deputy prior to leaving tonight. Well if that's not a sign that I am being promoted, I don't know what is. They recognise talent when they see it. They see that that I am a people person and a problem solver with an eye for detail. I think that statement just sums me up perfectly.

Gets all excited.

This is how it must have been for Sir Alex, or Fergie as we like to call him, and before him Sir Mat Busby. United recognised their brilliance and when the time was right moved them both upstairs, so to speak. Well I just know it, that time has come for me. (*Gets up from her chair.*) I'm being moved upstairs. It's onwards and upwards.

Fades.

Moving with the Times

Elizabeth is late fifties and a Conservative councillor in the North West of England; a position she has had for thirty-five years. She is also an active member of the local Women's Institute.

Setting

Scene 1 and 3: Armchair
Scene 2: Table and chair

Performance time:

10 minutes

Scene 1

Lights up.

Elizabeth sits in an armchair in her home.

Honestly all this change, I don't know how one is supposed to keep up with it all. If it's not the PC brigade demanding yet more concessions it's the boundary commission meddling in things they know little about.

Pause.

And what's behind all this rush for change? Well I'll tell you. The destruction of every fabric of society, everything that we hold dear. The wishes of the silent majority are just swept aside. My phone never stops ringing from concerned residents. Residents residing in the right area of the ward that is. Which is where my gripe with the Boundary Commission lies. Unelected do-good-ers. That's what they are.

Pause.

I've been doing a tremendous job for thirty-five years representing my ward. Never a word of discontent from a resident. Not one. Then out of the blue, driven by the PC brigade, the Boundary Commission decide to change the ward boundaries in an effort to ensure, as they put it, political wards are fairly balanced and represent the ever changing demographics of an area. Which putting it succinctly means, they don't want middle class wards like mine to thrive.

Pause.

So, they moved the top half of my ward into the adjacent one, which is run by three socialists. God forbid. I just can't help thinking about poor Mrs Philips who lives in that beautiful Georgian house in its own grounds having to seek help from the socialists. They'll probably make her turn her house into a commune for the homeless and refugees.

Pause.

And what did I get in return in this deal? Only a sink basin of a council estate. I ask you. I daren't set foot in the place. Grass verges and conservatories that's I what I deal with, not benefits and council housing lists. And complain! Boy can they complain. One woman rang me and said there's litter outside my house. I said, well why don't you go pick it up then. Another rang, only a young girl, single mother, you know the sort. She said she didn't understand the new benefit system, I said neither do I dear. That makes two of us.

Pause.

And don't get me started on the PC brigade. The primary school in the council estate asked me to attend their sports day. The constituency chair is a governor there, got a grandchild at the school I think. Anyway. Needs must, I accepted the invitation. Everything going as well as could be expected. Gave out a few medals and smiled a lot. Apparently what happens at the end is they have a mother and father race. Not in the same race you understand. One of the young girl's fathers only enters himself in the mother's race. Because he's one of those, I can't bear to even say the word, transgender people. Left this poor girl's mother to live with another bloke and is now having a gender realignment operation. I think it's called. Load of baloney if you ask me.

Pause.

So there he is on the start line with all the mothers. And what a surprise, when the whistle sounds, he's off like the clappers up the field and wins by a mile. No doubt he'll be back next year, when he's come to his senses and he'll be back in the father's race.

Pause.

Well he'll have a very interesting collection of trophies in his cabinet, that's for sure.

Pause.

I just despair sometimes, I really do.

Fades.

Scene 2

Lights up.

Elizabeth sits on a wooden chair in a room in the Guildhall. A picture of Margaret Thatcher hangs in the background.

I have just had another telling off by the chip whip of the Conservative group on the council. Yet another complaint from residents about my behaviour. No guesses from which area of the ward.

He said, 'Elizabeth you missed another surgery, last Saturday at the library, residents turned up.' I said yes and I put a sign up telling people that I could not attend and the staff at the library informed people. 'Were you ill?' he said. No, I said, I had a prior engagement. 'Would this prior engagement be attending the sale at Barker and Stonehouse?' he said. 'Because you were seen browsing by another resident.' The sale only lasts for one day I said, and I couldn't attend both. 'Priorities, Elizabeth, priorities.' What priorities, I thought, I got my priorities right. Never been a problem before me cancelling surgeries. My residents understood, they were usually at the store themselves.

Pause.

When I got home I was shocked to learn that one of the residents from the estate actually took it upon himself to come round to my house. One of the neighbours told me they saw a strange man wandering aimlessly around my garden, and had parked his Skoda outside my house. It was only when they confronted him that he told them the reason for his presence. He'd gone to the library, was told the surgery was cancelled so he took it upon himself to make a home visit. A Skoda. Really!

Pause.

I'd love to know who it was who saw me. They won't be from the council estate, I would have thought. They don't sell bric-a-brac at Barker and Stonehouse, the closest they'd get to the store is pressing their nose up against the window. It's more likely to be someone from the Constituency Party wanting to jump in my shoes. You get a lot of chumping at the heels in this game.

Pause.

Well it's been a week for complaints. I got contacted by the Chair of the WI a few days ago. I'm still shocked at the content of that discussion, quite frankly. To satisfy the PC brigade the WI set up an equality and diversity focus group, if you please.

Pause.

Its remit is to attract more minority groups into the organisation. Now we get every Tom, Dick and Harry joining the organisation. And when I say Tom, Dick and Harry, I am not exaggerating. Thanks to the PC brigade we now have a transgender bloke amongst our ranks. Sits there at our meetings as large as life, a great big sit footer in a skirt and blouse. Well thank you the equality and diversity focus group, you've made us the laughing stock. Wants to be involved in everything he said. Fantastic!

Pause.

And if that issue wasn't enough for the PC brigade; the chair of this new group approached me of all people. 'We have new members from the Asian community,' she said. 'They have passed their citizenship test but don't quite feel British.' Get them to learn the lines of *Land of Hope and Glory* I said. If they don't know the words to that off by heart they're not British.
Pause.

And that helpful bit of advice got me a ticking off from the Chair, with a threat that it might go higher.

Pause.

All these changes. One just can't keep up with it all. And what have some of these new recruits got to offer the organisation? Nothing is the answer. But if you offend them, they'll put a complaint in faster than you can blink. It's like walking on egg-shells to say the least.

Pause.

I was asked last week if I would help judge the baking contest. I've done it before, when the standard was extremely high. Some of those cakes could have gone on sale at some of the best stores in the country.

Pause.

So, I turned up to judge as I have done many times and there is our transgender friend, he's only one of the contestants. Supposedly he's going to bake a carrot cake. Hand's like a bunch of bananas he's got. He'd be better off on a building site than on a baking stall.

Pause.

The Chair suggested that we walk round and talk to each contestant fairly and equally, whatever that means. So I found myself eventually face to face with Mr Transgender. Carrot cake! You could have fooled me. It was flat hung over the side and caved in, in the middle. 'Say something positive,' whispered the Chair, as she walked past. Well, I said, thinking of Mary Berry. It's been on a bit of a journey. (*She puts her hand to the side of her mouth.*). A journey, it looked like it had been tied to the back of the 63 bus and dragged down the High Street.

Pause.

But we have to give constructive advice, according to the Chair. Equality and Diversity and all that.

Pause.

Where will it all end? I ask myself. Where will it all end?

Fades.

Scene 3

Lights up.

Elizabeth sits in an armchair in a Care Home. She is wearing a dressing gown.

'You need rest Elizabeth,' said my GP. 'I'm recommending to the Council that they find you a place in a care home for a fortnight, at least for respite.' The last few weeks have really taken their toll. The Chair of the local constituency came to see me and told me that the party would be seeking my deselection, and if that wasn't enough, the Chair of the Women's Institute rang me and said that they were looking at revoking my membership for inappropriate behaviour. So, here I am in a care home with every manner of people. Ex Dockers, postmen and building site workers. Not a professional amongst them. And as for the staff...

Pause.

They said when I came in here that I should treat my room as my own home. So I hung my picture of Margaret Thatcher up over my dressing table. Came back from lunch one day and it had gone. I wonder where that ended up. Probably in the bin I would have thought, along with all the values and decency that most of us hold dear.

Pause.

Sycamore Gardens they call this place, more like Sodom and Gomorrah if you ask me. When the HR department advertised for carers they must have stressed that they must be sexual deviants. Gays, lesbians, transgenders and wait for it, a gender fluid person. What in God's name I thought. The manager came to see me the other day to explain.

Pause.

She came into my room and sat in a chair opposite me. 'I need to speak to you on a very sensitive issue,' she said. 'Your carer Paul is sometimes Paula.' Come again I said. 'Paul is Gender Fluid, some days he feels male and some days he feels female. And we never know on a daily basis whether Paul or Paula is turning up for work,' she said. Gender Fluid. Well you could have knocked me down with a feather. There's no wonder the Council Tax is so high courtesy of the socialists, we're having to pay for double the uniforms for people like him. What does he do when he gets up in a morning I thought, flick a coin?

Pause.

Oh, I just despair. I really do.

Pause.

And if they don't know if it's Paul or Paula turning up for work. Neither does anybody else. Call him Paul when he's Paula or vice a versa and you'll probably end up sat in your armchair in the car park. It's PC gone mad, that's what it is, gone mad.

Pause.

I wonder whatever would happen if the Argies ever invaded again. It won't be a task force we send, it'll be more like the Transgender Express. When the drill sergeant enters the barracks, they'll be sat in front of the mirror combing their hair and applying their mascara. (*Exasperated.*) Oh I just despair.

Pause.

Well I'm not standing for it, someone's got to make a stand. There's no wonder the NHS is under such a strain. All this chopping and changing. Bits removed from people and probably stored in a jar somewhere, just in case they change their mind further down the road, and then it's back as you were, so to speak. All at the tax payers' expense of course. Well I'm putting a stop to it.

Pause.

It's patently obvious to me what the problem is – hormone imbalance. Males wanting to be females, females wanting to be male and even some who can't decide what they are. Hormone transfer is the answer. The NHS can swap hormones between the sexes. It'll stop all this nonsense and save the NHS millions.

Pause.

I shall be making my political comeback in the next few weeks. It's not a seat on the Council for me, it's Parliament. That's where I need to be. I'll be sending my application for approval to head office first thing in the morning. I'll write to the Chair of the national party, not the wet from the local constituency office. I want to be the main speaker at the next party conference. I'll knock them dead with my proposal, and I'll get a safe seat in the Home Counties. We'll have to up sticks. But needs must.

Pause.

It's not going to be grass verges and conservatories that I'll be remembered for. It's saving the NHS.

Pause.

Problem solving. That's always been my strong point. Putting two problems side by side and seeing how one can solve the other.

Pause.

It's what got me where I am today.

Fades.

The Queen of South Faxby

Stella is a retired international banker. She has moved to a small village in the North of England and sits on the parish council.

Setting

Scene 1: Table and chair
Scene 2: Wooden kitchen stool
Scene 3: Armchair

Performance time:

10 minutes

Scene 1

Lights up.

Stella sits behind a wooden table in the Village Hall.

Well it certainly hasn't been an easy time living in South Faxby. The problem here is that people are a bit stuck in their ways, not used to achieving. Everything seems to centre around farming, like it's the be all and end all, if you see what I mean.

I wanted a nice quiet life after the busy life I've had; jetting all over the world seeing business clients. I even jetted off one day to New York just for a lunch date with a client, and then hopped on the next flight home. Here, if people go to the local pub for a Sunday Roast they think it's a luxury. Well never mind, each to their own I suppose.

Pause.

Fortunately for everyone, I sit on the parish council and maybe I can influence life here a bit and bring the village into the 21st century.

I saw the vacancy for a parish councillor in the window of the local post office. The card read that a vacancy had arisen due to retirement and anyone interested should contact the clerk to the council. I contacted her straight away with my CV and she invited me to the council offices and there I met the Chair, nice man, landowner called Thomas, knew a thing or two about business.

They informed me that if no one else showed an interest by the end of the month, and there was only a week left, the position was mine. It was as simple as that. No need for an election. But then why would you need one? I am the best person for the role, no one else has my experience, and I can stay on the council for as long as I like, that's the rule. It's not like local authority councillors who have to go before the electorate every four years. But then they get paid. I do this job for the love of it, I have so much to offer.

Pause.

Thomas has been really busy just lately so he appointed me Deputy Chair. There wasn't anybody else really up to the role. Most of the other councillors are farmers except for Mrs Rodgers, who runs the local post office. Thomas just notified them by e-mail. It was placed as the first item on the agenda and it was a simple nod through.

Thomas then left the meeting and me to Chair in his absence. For somebody of my experience it was easy, like a duck to water. Everything was going well until we came to the last item on the agenda, the setting up of the flood committee.

The village had been substantially flooded last year when the river burst its banks. Thomas was severely affected by this as he owns most of the land in the village, most of the farmers are his tenants. All right most of the farmers had to put up with a little inconvenience, but events had a financial impact on Thomas as the landowner.

I, with my vast experience in the business world naturally thought that I should be the Chair. But the farmers didn't see it that way. They, along with Mrs Rogers only tried to usurp proceedings and attempted to put Roy, farmer, as Chair of the committee. They argued that he should be Chair as the farm that he rents from Thomas was knee deep in water. Well you could have knocked me down with a feather. What experience is that? Chair indeed. I could see that if I put it to the vote they would vote Roy in.

I used my business brain and adjourned the meeting until the next week, Chair's prerogative. I phoned Thomas as soon as I got home and told him what had occurred. Within minutes of our discussion he phoned me back and uttered those marvellous words, 'all sorted.' It was like music to my ears. If only they had seen sense in the first place we wouldn't have to all have had to come back the following week.

Pause.

The Environment Agency invited the environment minister to the village to inspect the flood plans that they had drawn up to prevent a similar incident. The Environment Agency informed the parish council through the secretary of the visit. When I became aware of this breach of protocol, I immediately contacted the secretary at the town hall and requested very firmly that she writes to the Environment Agency reminding them of the protocol, and that I as Chair of the flood committee and Deputy Chair of the Parish Council should be notified of such a visit well in advance. Needless to say we didn't get a response.

Pause.

I contacted a journalist from the local newspaper and informed them that I would be in attendance for the visit in my capacity as Chair of the flood committee. I informed her that I would be available for interview at any time prior to the visit and on the day itself. I gave her my contact details. I wrote to the minister asking if he would meet with me when he attends. Not sure if he even read my letter, I got a response from a Sir Humphry informing that he had a very busy schedule etc, etc.

Pause.

I received no phone call or e-mail from the journalist and was unable to contact her when I tried to ring. A colleague always answered telling me that she was away from her desk and would contact me on her return. Never did. The day of the visit came, officers from the Environment Agency everywhere. The minister came surrounded by civil servants, the local MP was there, I didn't even know he was coming and the three local authority councillors, ditto. None of these people even had the courtesy to drop me a line to let me know of their attendance. Manners seem to be non-existent in this place.

Pause.

And as for the local journalist, she milked the day for all it was worth, I've no doubt it will look good on her CV; interviewing the minister and the local MP. No time for me. She came with a photographer who took photographs throughout the day. When I purchased the paper the next day I was in one photograph, you could just make me out in the background, stood behind the minister and the MP. Absolute disgrace.

Fades.

Scene 2

Lights up.

Stella sits on a wooden chair kitchen stool in her home.

Sometimes I feel that people in the village just haven't accepted me into the fold. When I moved into the village, to start off with I lived in one of the Thomas's rented properties whilst I had a new build erected. I saw some land available near the post office opposite a farm. There had not been a new build in the village for a number of years, so all the houses looked the same. All red brick, rather dull really. I wanted mine to be vibrant and modern whilst blending in with the local area. I instructed the architect to build a modern building, mainly glass, but the roof to be of a cow shed design to fit in with the farm across the road. Well blow me, there were objections galore when it went before the planning committee. Luckily it went through on appeal. Some people just don't like change.

Pause.

At least one person in the area seems to like me and appreciates what I can do. Julie, from the next village, retired head teacher, my sort of person. Informed me at a function that we were both attending that she was approaching her 60th birthday in a few months' time. What are you doing to celebrate? I asked. 'I haven't got anything planned as yet,' she replied. Well I couldn't let the opportunity go astray. I am an excellent organiser I told her, and gave her examples from my work history. I could see she was impressed. I got her details and contacted her the next day to confirm that I would organise the day for her. We just needed to set a price per head. I suggested that we meet at a certain eatery in another village to go through the finer details. I always like to do things properly.

Pause.

Thomas very kindly offered to take us to the eatery as the venue was on the way to an engagement that he had. But he wouldn't be able to bring us back as he did not know when he would be finished. He said he would pick us both up at my house at 19.00 hours. He always uses the twenty-four hour system, he used to be an officer in the South African army. He emigrated to this country during the uprising and he had his land confiscated by the black people, so he came here with his wealth and invested in the village. Not that anyone round here thinks of thanking him.

Pause.

Well I just had time to nip to the local public house just round the corner from me. Not for a drink you understand. The pub has got a new landlord and I had been the previous Sunday for Sunday lunch. The food wasn't cooked in the way that I thought it should have been, the meat a little tough and the vegetables a little on the dry side. So, I thought I would go round and give them a few tips.

I asked politely to speak to David, the landlord. He came out with his wife. I delicately raised the issue of the meal and ex-plained that he needed to get things right or his business plans would fail. Well, what a commotion. Out of the kitchen came the cook, utensils in hand. 'What's wrong with my cooking,' she said. It's just a bit of constructive criticism, I said. I tried to explain in the nicest possible way that her cooking wasn't quite up to the standard that one expects and is, indeed, use to.

You would think that someone in her position would appreci-ate some help and advice from a world travelled person like myself, someone who is a bit of an expert on world cuisine. I tried to tell her about my jaunt to New York for lunch, but she wasn't prepared to listen. Poor thing, she probably has never even been to York never mind New York. She started shouting and waving her hands about. Next thing I knew I was been asked to leave. Never been treated like it before in my life.

Pause.

We arrived at the eatery just on time. Julie was a little late getting to my place. Said she was stuck behind a tractor on route. Well better late than never, I always say.

A young man showed us to our table. I said to him where is the menu, we don't appear to have one. 'Madam,' he said, 'it's a surprise menu.' Come again I said. 'It's a surprise menu,' he said. Well what's on it? I said. 'I'm not allowed to tell you,' he said. Well, what a carry on. He passed us both a wine menu. How are we supposed to order wine when I don't know what I am eating? I said. White wine goes with certain meals and red with another. Everyone knows that. He still wouldn't let on, anyone would think he was a captured spy and was refusing to divulge information during interrogation. In the end he ended up picking the wine. What a carry on.

Pause.

The meal was brought through and after all the suspense it turned out to be chicken. Where has the chicken come from? I said. 'From the kitchen,' he said. I mean where was it sourced? I said. 'it is locally sourced,' he said. How local? I said. 'I don't know,' he said. Well can you find out? I said. He disappeared into the kitchen, came back and said, 'a local farmer.' Which local farmer? I said. 'I don't know', he said. 'Does it matter?' Of course it matters, I said. Go and find out. I said to Julie, it had better not be from the farm down the road, he doesn't look after the birds he keeps, I'm surprised he hasn't been closed down, the place is totally unhygienic. The waiter came back and said, neither he nor the chef knew and the owner was away. Well what a performance. I know the owner and I will speak to him on his return. He needs to know how his business is being run in his absence.

Pause.

Well, I brought up the issue with Julie as to how much she wanted to spend per head on her party. '£60.00 per head,' she said. You won't get much for that I said. (*Puts hand to one side of mouth and whispers.*) I realised money was an issue so I didn't push it. (*Normal voice.*) Well £60.00 per head it is I said, very diplomatically. Could be shopping at Aldi's I thought.

Pause.

The evening came to an end. I paid with my card and left a reasonable tip. We would like a taxi, I said to the receptionist. And when you ring make sure the driver isn't one of those East Europeans in a Lada. They drive like maniacs, I said. 'We can't stipulate who the driver is or what vehicle they drive,' she said. It's PC gone mad if you ask me.

Pause.

The day of the party came and I was organised as usual. I arrived early in the morning with a young girl from the village. She's just starting college in a few weeks' time, and she was glad of the money. I managed to stay within budget somehow, had to be very shrewd. (*Lets off a laugh.*)

So I managed to pay her £15.00 for a morning's work. Very rewarding, she'll gain a lot of experience working with me, I thought. We had everything spick and spam, but then the guests started to arrive. I had stipulated on the invites to arrive no earlier than 30 minutes before the official start. I had set up a little bar in the garage and that was the route through to the garden, which is where the party was being held. The early arrivers only thought that they could have a drink on arrival. No you cannot, I said. The bar opens at the start of the event and not before.

Pause.

Sometimes, one has to be firm.

Fades.

Scene 3

Lights up.

Stella sits in an armchair in her home.

It's been a very eventful last few days, I must say. I decided to hold an exhibition of my pottery and fabrics that I have collected over many years. When I have been globetrotting around the world I have collected porcelain etc from every country. I have built up quite a collection. It's not possible in my new home to have everything on display, so I hit on the idea of hiring a studio in the town down the road. I wanted everyone in the area to have the opportunity to see pottery and fabric from around the world. These people here are not great travellers you see. Some have never even been to the next village. I advertised the event in the local paper and placed an advert in the post office window.

Pause.

I was really looking forward to the event. I was in the post office sending out invites to some important people I know in London. When a local farmer, who attends the parish council meetings, stood before me in his Wellington boots and said, 'So you're exhibiting your cloths and pots and pans.' Words just failed me, which believe me is a rare event. Don't these people want culture? I asked myself.

Pause.

The night before the exhibition I arranged for a little soirée at my place for selected guests, Thomas being one of them. Influential people mainly. One or two people from London came, people I used to work with. However, a bit disappointed with the local turnout. Thomas was at a prior engagement and the local councillor's did not even have the courtesy to RSVP. I knew one invite wasn't coming, he RSVP'd in no uncertain terms.

I met David at a networking session for local business people. Thought I would give people the benefit of my expertise. David runs a shop selling furniture and bric a brac. We got on as soon as we were introduced. We had a few dinner dates and I gave him some sound business advice. It was at one of these dinner dates that he informed me he was gay. Not a problem I said. I thought he should move to London, the place is full of them.

Anyway, I thought I would help him by purchasing certain items of interest that he could either sell or hold on to, if he really liked it. I always know people's tastes, just a skill you pick up in my line of business. If I see something, I purchased it and then arranged delivery to his shop with a little note attached thus: thought you would like this. S. X.

Well, I was out browsing the shops when I saw a lovely draylon sofa. It was in pink, never thought it would be a problem. I purchased and dispatched with my usual message. He sent my card invite back with a message written on the back declining to attend and saying something about stereotyping. He also told me never to contact him again. It doesn't take much to offend some people.

Pause.

I had to go round to the neighbours, inviting people on the day. I'd hoped they realised it was a formal occasion, and would turn up suitably dressed. It would have been embarrassing for my friends if they were suited and booted and the locals turned up in Wellington boots. Well no one turned up in the latter, however, someone did ask for a can of lager. As if?

Pause.

So the next day I got up early to go to the exhibition, I thought better be there when everyone arrives so I can explain the origins of everything on display. There were cards giving some explanation, but I thought it would be an opportunity for the attendees to gain a bit more knowledge and to meet the person responsible for the exhibition.

Pause.

I was just getting ready to go when there was a knock on the door. When I opened it, two RSPCA officers were present. One was at my door, the other was looking through the window of an annex that I had specially built for my two cats. Two beautiful cats they are. I didn't want any old moggie, I wanted a breed. I purchased two Bengal cats that I found on the Internet. 'We have had a complaint about the way your cats are kept,' said one of the officers. The other one who was peering through the glass said, 'it looks totally unhygienic to me. We need to inspect further.' They came into my house, went straight into the glass room and said that there was not enough ventilation and it was unhygienic. Well, that's the fault of the architects, I said. And I offered to show them the letters I had sent to the architect complaining. They weren't interested. They took Teemot and Tilly away. They said that I would have to contact them in a week's time and they would come and inspect the premises again. Apparently it was the breeder who had made the complaint. She had called un-expectantly and peered through the glass, and then had the gall to speak to the neighbours, and they told her that they never come out.

Pause.

I might have known a neighbour would be involved somewhere along the line. They can't deal with someone who is successful.

Pause.

The event was hardly a success. Very low turnout. Friends from London attended and fortunately stayed all day. Not many locals even bothered to come. Maybe they just don't understand culture. Maybe they are just too busy in their own little worlds.

Pause.

Maybe I'm a little too sensitive for this village.

Pause.

Maybe when I get Teemot and Tilly back I'll move away.

Fades.